To

From

Date

Cheryl Karpen

A little book to nurture your soul

hope for a
hurting heart

THOMAS NELSON
Since 1978

NASHVILLE   DALLAS   MEXICO CITY   RIO DE JANEIRO

Dedicated to the people who opened the
door to my store, Something Different,
and who tenderly walked into my heart.

Every experience God gives
us, every person He puts
in our lives, is the perfect
preparation for the future in
which only He can see.

Corrie ten Boom

Introduction

I have learned that we grieve many losses in our lives.

This book is about my first experience with the kind of loss that felt devastating to me. It is also about the story of what I learned from my loss and how I evolved into a stronger person from it. I share this story with you because, for some reason, others have found my steps through grief helpful in their own recovery process. When they hear my yesterday's story and see who I am today, it seems to inspire them and encourage them even more.

If someone had told me that sometimes we need brokenness in order to become whole again, I would not have understood. But along my road of healing, I gathered some truly precious touchstones of wisdom that are what make me whole today. Some were discovered from my own experiences. Some are what I learned by watching and listening to others. With their blessing, I have included pieces of their stories to share with you as well.

I hope these touchstones affirm you, encourage you, and, in time, help you to soar.

Cheryl Karpen

Today, I will give
myself a BIG hug.

I was a vivacious and spirited woman. Many people envied my spontaneity, freedom, and optimism in the face of risks. I had lived in foreign countries and traveled to exotic places. I owned my own business—one I had started—and thrived on the autonomy it gave me. I chased dreams and flourished as they came true. And I was in love with a charming, handsome man.

To make matters sweeter still, I was surrounded by a loving family and friends. In fact it was to them that I freely gave advice. Even when they didn't ask for it.

You see, I thought I knew how to "do life."

Then suddenly, my world went dark. Without warning, my relationship with that charming, handsome man—the one I believed to be the love of my life—ended abruptly.

So very abruptly.

I am a compassionate
and loving person.

All those things people say about having the wind knocked out of you are true. Abandoned and reeling, I found myself under an avalanche of grief. My search for answers was relentless . . . "Why me, Lord? Will I ever be happy again? How do I end this heartache?"

In my distress I called upon the LORD,
And cried out to my God. . . .

Psalm 18:6

Today I will ask for help.

Cast your cares on the LORD and he will sustain you;
he will never let the righteous fall.

Psalm 55:22 NIV

As the sole employee of my gift shop, my responsibilities hadn't come to an end simply because it felt like my life had. And so I unlocked the doors each day and tried to greet each customer with a smile.

But my heartache was too great to hide. My regular customers were the first to notice. They missed the light in my eyes, the playfulness in my step. Puzzled and concerned, they dared to ask, "Are you okay?"

Their compassion was not what I expected. And it was a tenderness I couldn't refuse. Disarmed by their genuine concern, I opened my heart. I told them why I hurt. And when they reached out, I literally fell into their arms.

I am rich in hope and spirit.

They held me with their understanding. They embraced my sadness as their own. And they shared their own stories—stories of loss and heartbreak. They talked about the loss of a spouse. The tragic loss of a child. Sister. Brother. Mother or father.

They talked about other losses too . . . a career ended without explanation; the diagnosis we so dread; the elusiveness of hope; the vulnerability of faith; the loss of a dream.

I no longer felt alone.

I felt as if God had surrounded me with guardian angels, human angels who took me under their wings and helped me believe better days would come. Ironically, these angels were also my customers who came to me looking to buy a gift.

I am grateful for all the blessings in my life.

Let your unfailing love
surround us, LORD,
for our hope is in you alone.

Psalm 33:22 NLT

Instead, they were the givers and the gift was mine . . . the gift of hope.

In time, the ache in me subsided. My broken heart began to mend in spite of my certainty that it would never be whole again. And as I emerged—a little wiser and undeniably stronger—so did my business.

There was a new focus, a new clarity to the purpose with which I stocked my shelves. I was drawn to messages and merchandise that affirmed people as worthy and deserving. I sought out gifts that nurtured the heart and touched lives with hope and healing and growth.

It was as if my entire world was new, RE-created from the inside out. And I had a mission. It became my passion to create a place of sanctuary and serenity for others who were in need of hope and healing. I wanted to give back to others what my customers, my family, and my friends had so generously given to me.

I am so grateful for **ALL** the lessons I have learned.

Experience is a gifted teacher if we are willing to learn. Through my journey, and later when I was able to look back with a clearer heart and mind, I recorded the lessons I learned so I could help someone else—you—the way others so graciously helped me. It is my hope that you will draw something from my experience that will take you another step closer toward a world of comfort and blessing for this day.

I learned that feelings of grief and loss are part of everyone's life. No one escapes them. And while we can't control these experiences, it is one of life's great discoveries that we can make choices about how to deal with them.

I found out, to my great surprise, that loss of one kind often becomes a lightning rod for other, earlier losses. At first, I was puzzled by the magnitude of my grief over a lost love. After all, I knew people who had suffered multiple deaths in a single day. In comparison, mine was a relatively small tragedy; and yet, I was completely undone.

So I rejoice and am glad.
Even my body has hope. . . .

Psalm 16:9 NCV

Today I will live with
hope in my heart.

Then I began to remember . . . the death of my father years before. The death of my nephew. These were profound losses to me. They were also ones that I had not been ready, or willing, to grieve earlier. I think I was afraid they would hurt too much. And I was right.

Which was the beginning of my next discovery: THERE IS NO SUB-STITUTE FOR GRIEVING. Nor is there an easy way out. We may think that burying feelings we don't know quite what to do with will make them go away. But then, one day, something stirs that reservoir and without warning, all that raw emotion we had forgotten erupts like a volcano. Fiercely. Uncontrollably. And we begin to wonder if we'll ever emerge from the ruins or savor the sunshine again.

I am enough just the way I am.

I am fearfully and wonderfully made....

Psalm 139:14

I learned that where there's grief in abundance, depression isn't far behind. The trouble is a person living with depression is often the last one to recognize it. If you experience repeated bouts of hopelessness or your sadness becomes an Arctic winter in duration, depression is at work. Seeking professional help—whether from a family doctor, a psychologist, or a pastor—can be sunshine to someone who only sees darkness. Your life is much too worthy and precious to live forever in sadness. Be willing to ask for help if you need it.

I learned that significant loss often includes a "loss of self." Many of us travel through life validating our self-worth through relationships, jobs, and external sources that include everything from prestige to possessions. But *we* are not these things. Each of us is an individual, unique and unrepeatable. *Each day* we need to affirm how worthy we are, simply for who we are.

Today I will love
and honor myself.

I came to understand that no matter how much you love someone, you cannot control anyone else's life, their health, or the decisions they make. You can, however, take charge of your own life. Learning to love yourself and respect your needs will help you become strong again—both physically and emotionally.

I learned that we can choose to reach out and accept the help people offer us, or we can push them away.

I learned (and this one took me a while) that we can remain stuck in the past and anxious about the future. Or, we can try to live in the present moment . . . one hour and one day at a time.

I discovered firsthand why the saying "Let Go and Let God" has given so many others the courage to face another day. Although letting go is one of life's most difficult challenges, it is also one of life's most liberating lessons. Put simply: have the grace to give up what has been *for what could be*.

Today I will try to do one
thing that will make a
positive impact on my life.

I learned that we can become better, or we can become bitter. I have my friend Esther to thank for this wisdom. After hearing her story about the loss of a young child, I know what choice she made. You can see it in her eyes and feel it in her kind, compassionate heart. With her story to inspire me, I began to see that I really did have choices—even when it felt like there weren't any. Some days that choice was as simple as changing my attitude or surrendering my grief to God.

I learned I could choose to take baby steps toward healing or I could get lost in self-pity (and miss for all time the wonder of a sunrise or the comfort of coffee with a friend).

And, most importantly, I have learned:

We are all worthy and deserving of love in our lives.

Today I will believe in myself.
AGAIN.

Watch for it! Love comes to us in many different ways . . . through a friend, a child, a sibling, a parent, a grandparent, an aunt, an uncle, a pet, and always from our heavenly Father.

SO NOW THE QUESTION IS:

What can you do to make this challenging time in your life a little less painful? What can you do to be kinder and gentler to yourself?

Give yourself permission to experience all of those feelings you don't know what to do with. There is nothing wrong with you. You have faced a great loss and need time to heal.

Surround yourself with people who make you feel good about yourself. Seek out and nurture friendships that are positive and encouraging.

I am so much more
than my body.
I am spirit. I am heart.

Observe and become aware of how nature's gifts keep RE-generating around you. Trees lose their leaves in the fall and new buds appear in the spring. Flowers die off only to bloom again and again. Caterpillars turn into magnificent butterflies. Watch and listen. You, too, will once again thrive and grow.

Eavesdrop on your "self-talk." Negative, disparaging, and hopeless thoughts only erode the spirit. Determine to replace them with positive affirmations.

"Every day in every way
I get better and better and better."

"I am a worthy and deserving person."

This may take some practice, but don't give up. Most good things do!

Today I will give myself
permission to be sad.

Forgive yourself for everything you did—and didn't—do! Learn to accept yourself as one big, lovable, imperfect, and perfectly human being.

Congratulate yourself on making it through another day! Buy yourself a treat. Give yourself a hug. Spend time doing something you love. You deserve it.

Treat yourself as you would your own best friend. Talk to yourself with love, praise, and encouragement. (After all, who knows you better than the person you are affirming?)

Share in other people's stories of loss. Not only will you discover that you are not alone, but their stories will help you take heart. Don't be surprised if they even help you recognize new strength and courage in yourself.

Today I will make a list of all the things I enjoy doing. Maybe I will try to do one of them.

Get busy! Exercise. Go back to work. Take a class. Join a Bible study. It will get your mind engaged on something other than your situation. Reach out and help others through volunteer work. Your kindness will come back to you in countless ways.

Keep a gratitude journal. Each day, spend a few moments jotting down something you are grateful for:

A SPECIAL FRIEND
A PRAYER ANSWERED
MAKING IT THROUGH THE NIGHT
A BEAUTIFUL SUNSET
CLEAN SHEETS
A FLOWER
A SMILE
A PHONE CALL

Putting your thoughts and feelings on paper is healing. One day you will be able to look back and see how far you have come.

Today I will have trust and faith in the future.

But one thing I do, forgetting those thing
which are behind and reaching forward t
those things which are ahead .

Philippians 3:

Know that you are a somebody—no matter your age, your marital status, your education, or your income.

You are a *somebody*, a very important and worthy somebody. You are a gift to this world with a unique purpose and life all your own.

No one can take away your history, your memories, your pain, your joy, and all the ways in which your life here has so beautifully touched others. It is yours! Recognize and *celebrate* how special you are.

You are a survivor. You are a kind and loving person, a child of God, and a very important *somebody*. No one, absolutely no one, can take your significance away.

I am never alone.

"I will never leave you
nor forsake you."

Hebrews 13:5

Our lives, like stories, have a beginning, a middle, and an end. Once I felt as if mine was over. And it is true that loss marks an end of something dear. But (and here's the most amazing part) it is not the end of *your* story—your very own, irrepressible, still-in-the-works life story.

And the loss that started me on this journey? There is still an ache. There always will be.

But I continue to grow because of it. And, best of all, I don't have to grow alone! Family, friends, and God's grace and mercy are living reminders of the support and encouragement by which we mend broken hearts and fill empty places.

One spring morning remains vivid in my mind.

Today I will surrender
my grief to GOD.

Particularly consumed by my sadness, I sat curled up in a chair sobbing when my mother walked into the room. She gently placed her arms around me and tenderly whispered in my ear, "Don't worry. God just has a different plan for you."

Today, I look back at that moment many years ago, and I am in awe of her wisdom and her knowing. Whenever I am in doubt about my life, those wise words have a way of slipping back into my mind.

Don't give up *hope*.

Have faith.

Have trust.

Have patience.

God has a plan for you, too. My wise and precious mother told me so.

Today I will spend quiet
time in prayer.

LITTLE STORIES
OF HOPE AND HEALING

At the age of forty-nine, Kathy still finds comfort in stroking something soft and fuzzy—a buttery soft stuffed animal—that was with her during a family crisis and the subsequent death of her father. Today, that same stuffed animal not only reminds her of healing through loss, but it also reminds her that she is a survivor.

Ohrn, who lost his beloved wife after fifty-five years of marriage, brings delight to his neighbors every spring. He tends his garden of colorful tulips with passion, and brings the joy of renewal and beauty to an entire community.

Today I will do something
nice for myself.

Gene was middle-aged when a crisis hit his long-term marriage. Out of the self-doubt and rejection, he began sharing his pain with people who were important to him. To his amazement, an outpouring of love and support followed him—and with it, the courage to face an uncertain future.

Divorced, Lucy joined a women's support group where she met others who could empathize with her situation. After a time of healing, Lucy the Conservative became Lucy the Risk Taker. She left the comfort of family and friends in the suburbs, moved to the city, and never looked back.

Today I will give
myself permission to be happy.

Darlene, who has lost a child, battled cancer, and lives with congestive heart failure, lives optimistically. When asked how she maintains such a positive attitude, she replied, "Whenever I begin to feel sorry for myself, I think of all the people in the world who have much greater problems and hardships."

Gina finds comfort in quiet moments. After she puts her three boys to bed, she likes to draw a warm bath with lots of bubbles, read an inspirational book, pray, and meditate.

Today I will take a walk
among the trees.

At the age of fifty-eight, Julia felt alone after her best friend, her husband, died. Although many of her "couple" friends would continue to include her in activities, she often felt like a third or fifth person. Julia's life changed dramatically after she met Marion, also a widow. Together they travel to the local theater for an afternoon matinee or as far away as Nova Scotia for a new experience.

During a painful divorce, Barb began weekly visits to the local florist to have fresh flowers refilled in her small vase. The flowers symbolize a new beginning for Barb and remind her that life can be filled with beauty and wonder.

Today I will begin to live
in the present moment.

Friday nights were difficult for Beth following the breakup of a serious relationship. After all, Friday night was date night. Realizing this, one Friday night, a caring friend invited her to go horseback riding. Fridays became a standing engagement at the ranch. Beth renewed her passion for riding, and refreshed her spirit through connecting with the natural beauty that surrounded her.

After the death of her husband, Jeri became a hospice volunteer. Later she went on to volunteer at a local elementary school where she helps first-graders with their reading. Today at the age of seventy-nine, she works at a gift shop at least two days a week and has become Main Street's favorite mom.

Grant me the grace to
embrace my life.

Growing up, Nora lived in several different countries. Change became a way of life and new situations proved an endless source of interest. But when the last of Nora's three children left home, she was totally unprepared for the avalanche of loneliness that followed. To her surprise, it was the solitude of a nearby nature center that provided comfort. To this day when she feels lonely, Nora finds solace in nature during long walks among the trees.

Duty isn't a word we hear much today. But for Darren it was heartfelt duty that helped him survive a time of betrayal and extreme pain. For him the countermeasure for overwhelming chaos was finding hope in spiritual—rather than material—fulfillment. "Life as we know it is pretty temporary. But eternity's forever. Remember who you are and *whose* you are, and that *you are loved*."

The following pages are reserved for personal
thoughts and affirmations.

Ways in which I can be kinder
and gentler with myself:

....

....

....

....

....

....

Things I have to look forward to:

....

....

....

....

....

....

....

....

....

....

Things I am grateful for:

Scripture and quotes that have helped me most:

....

....

....

....

....

....

....

A Note from the Author

One Last Lesson

For a long time I hesitated to publish *Hope for a Hurting Heart*. And rightly so. Exposing my innermost thoughts and revisiting painful ground is more vulnerable than I care to be these days.

I also questioned the significance of my pain when compared to others whose loss seemed to be much greater. What did I have to say that could grace their lives with hope?

Dear friends thought otherwise. The circumstances that plunge us into grief are all worthy of validation, they reminded me. And the multitude of ways in which we grieve? They are matched by a thousand ways in which we learn to take—and give—comfort along the way. And so I began to put my hand—and heart—on paper.

Thanks to an entire team of caring, compassionate cheerleaders—family and friends—their words of encouragement and kind acts of support, this book moved from my heart into your hands. I thank all of you who cheered me on, especially during those times when it felt as if there was nothing in life to cheer about. Today, I treasure life, and most of all I treasure all of you.

Also, a most heartfelt thanks to all the individuals who trusted me enough to share their stories, my editors, Lisa Stilwell and Susan Foust, and to the entire team at Thomas Nelson Publishers who work tirelessly to bring messages of hope and faith to the world.

And lastly, a special HEART FULL of gratitude to my amazing mother, Julia C. Karpen, for always, always believing.

Blessings,

Cheryl Karpen

You might also benefit from
these additional sources of hope . . .

Jesus Calling and *Jesus Lives* by **Sarah Young**

Safe in the Shepherds Arms and *Live Loved* by **Max Lucado**

God's Shelter for Your Storm by **Sheila Walsh**

Looking Up When Life Is Looking Down Devotional Journal by **Beth Moore**

Deeper Than Tears

Sanctuary by **David Jeremiah**

The Butterfly Effect by **Andy Andrews**

God's Promises by **Jack Countryman**